Tablets

Also by Dunya Mikhail

Poetry
In Her Feminine Sign
The Iraqi Nights
Fifteen Iraqi Poets (editor)
Diary of a Wave Outside the Sea
The War Works Hard

Fiction
The Bird Tattoo

Nonfiction
The Beekeeper: Rescuing the Stolen Women of Iraq

Tablets:
Secrets of the Clay

Dunya Mikhail

A New Directions Paperbook Original

Acknowledgments: Tremendous thanks to Jeffrey Yang for his meticulous editing of this book; to Charlotte Seymour, my literary agent, for her wise guidance; and to Lori Cohen, my friend who has supported me from the moment I arrived in this country—her kindness has been an inspiration.

Some of these poems first appeared in the following publications: *The Best American Poetry 2023*, *Modern Poetry in Translation*, *Poetry*, and *The Nation*.

"Tablets I" was translated by Kareem James Abu-Zeid and originally appeared in *The Iraqi Nights* (2014). "Tablets II–V" originally appeared in *In Her Feminine Sign* (2019).

Manufactured in the United States of America
First published as a New Directions Paperbook (NDP1609) in 2024
Book design by Eileen Bellamy

Library of Congress Cataloging-in-Publication Data
Names: Mīkhāʾīl, Dunyā, 1965– author. | Abu-Zeid, Kareem James, translator.
Title: Tablets : secrets of the clay / Dunya Mikhail, with drawings by the author.
Description: First edition. | New York : New Directions Publishing Corporation, 2024.
Identifiers: LCCN 2024024869 | ISBN 9780811237970 (trade paperback) |
ISBN 9780811237987 (ebook)
Subjects: LCGFT: Poetry.
Classification: LCC PJ7846.1392 T33 2024 | DDC 892.7/16—dc23/eng/20240625
LC record available at https://lccn.loc.gov/2024024869

10 9 8 7 6 5 4 3 2 1

New Directions Books are published for James Laughlin
by New Directions Publishing Corporation
80 Eighth Avenue, New York 10011

ndbooks.com

To Khatoun, my mother, who says
"only love saves the world"

To Mazin, my husband, who cries tears of joy
when he hears a good poem

To Larsa, my daughter, whose Sumerian
name is inscribed on my heart

Contents

Author's Note

At this moment, I am writing to you using a tablet such as a computer, or iPad, or cellphone. If I were living in the time before writing, I would express my thoughts to you through clay tablets. I would draw my ideas the way my Sumerian ancestors used to do thousands of years ago. This is, in fact, exactly what I set out to do in this book. I imagined myself living during that time without an alphabet, needing to record my poetry through drawing.

Never learning how to formally draw served me well in this book, as these drawings are supposed to be "primitive," being in harmony with the spirit of those simple signs that communicated with the world for the first time. After all, those ancestors of mine couldn't all be artists. I like to think that many of them were ordinary people who revealed a part of themselves through the symbols they inscribed on cave walls and clay tablets. I am fascinated by their codes, which are lyrical without intentionally being so. I wonder what they wanted to say when they drew an eye, a hand, a fish, or a bird, for example? Were those images representations of the objects themselves, or metaphors for other things? What does a circle mean? The world, or infinity, or a wheel, or time? An expression of love and renewal, isolation and hope? Starting all over from zero?

I practiced at least two layers of translation in *Tablets*: the first from words in one language, Arabic, to another, English; and the second from words to images. Sometimes the poems seemed to be written in both languages simultaneously.

What I received from my ancestors are offerings of the future rather than of the past. Now it's my turn to offer them to you.

Tablets I

I

She pressed her ear against the shell:
she wanted to hear everything
he never told her.

2

A single inch
separates their two bodies
facing one another
in the picture:
a framed smile
buried beneath the rubble.

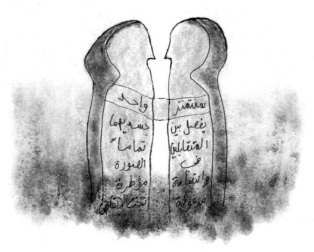

3

Whenever you throw stones
into the sea
it sends ripples through me.

4

My heart's quite small—
that's why it fills so quickly.

5
Water needs no effort
to mix with water
and fill the blank spaces.

6
The tree doesn't ask why it's not moving
to some other forest
nor any other pointless questions.

7

He watches TV
while she holds a novel.
On the novel's cover
there's a man watching TV
and a woman holding a novel.

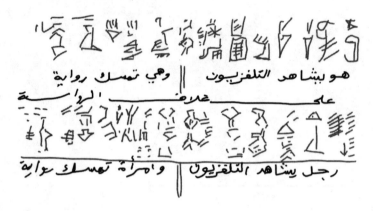

8

On the first morning
of the new year
all of us will look up
at the same sun.

9
He fell dead:
a star twinkles in the dust.

10
The person who gazed at me for so long,
and whose gaze I returned for just as long . . .
That man who never once embraced me,
and whom I never once embraced . . .
The rain wrecked the colors around him
on that old canvas.

11

He wasn't with the husbands
who were lost and then found;
he didn't come with the prisoners of war,
nor with the kite that took her,
in her dream,
to some other place,
while she stood before the camera
to have her smile
glued into the passport.

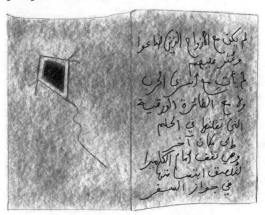

12

Dates piled high
beside the road:
your way
of kissing me.

13

Rapunzel's hair
reaching down
from the window
to the earth
is how we wait.

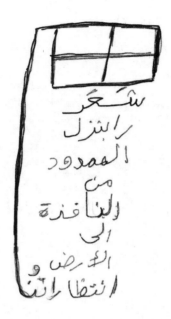

14

The shadows
the prisoners left
on the wall
surrounded the jailer
and cast light
on his loneliness.

15

Homeland, I am not your mother,
so why do you weep in my lap like this
every time
something hurts you?

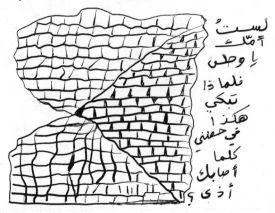

16

Never mind this bird—
it comes every day
and stops at the branch's edge
to sing for an hour
or two.
That's all it does:
nothing else makes it happier.

17
House keys,
identity cards,
faded pictures among the bones . . .
All of these are scattered
in a single mass grave.

18
The Arabic language
loves long sentences
and long wars.
It loves neverending songs
and late nights
and weeping over ruins.

19
Far away from home—
that's all that changed in us.

20
Cinderella left her slipper in Iraq
along with the smell of cardamom
wafting from the teapot,
and that huge flower,
its mouth gaping like death.

21
Instant messages
ignite revolutions.
They spark new lives
waiting for a country to download,
a land that's little more
than a handful of dust
when faced with these words:
"There are no results that match your search."

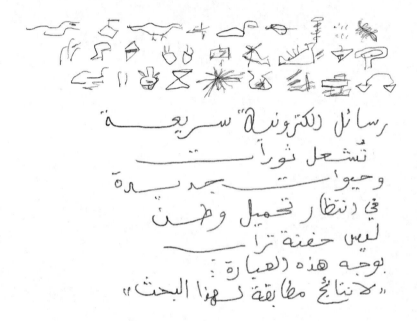

22

The dog's excitement
as he brings the stick to his owner
is the moment of opening the letter.

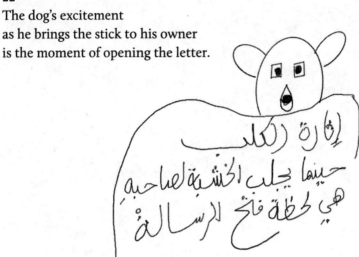

23

We cross borders lightly
like clouds.
Nothing carries us,
but as we move on
we carry rain,
and an accent,
and a memory
of another place.

24

How thrilling to appear in his eyes.
She can't understand what he's saying:
she's too busy chewing his voice.
She looks at the mouth she'll never kiss,
at the shoulders she'll never cry on,
at the hands she'll never hold,
and at the ground where their shadows meet.

كم مثير أن نظهر في عينيه

لا تفهم ما يقوله لها

مشغولة بمضغ صوته في فمها

تنظر إلى فمه الذي لن تقبّله

إلى كتفيه التي لن تبكي فوقها

إلى يده التي لن تمسكها

إلى الأرض حيث ظلاهما يلتقيان

Tablets II

1

I close my eyes and I see a dot.
It becomes a spot of light.
It grows into the size of a person
who moves into the distances
until it returns to a spot of light,
a dot.

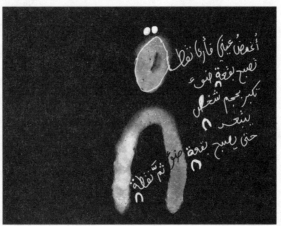

2

Like communion bread
your words dissolve in my mouth
and never die.

3
I don't care under which sky—
just sing your song till the end.

4
The bone city I am choked by
is also salt
also sugar
also boiling water
in the kettle without a lid.

5

Ask not how many houses were built.
Ask how many residents remained in the houses.

6

The flame opens like a giant plant
swallowing them one by one
with their lost-and-found sheep.

7
She whose song
has no beginning
or end;
she whose voice
faded into stars and moons . . .
Where is she?
Where is she?

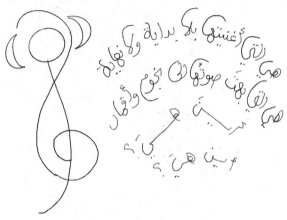

8
Do you have a manual
for fixing the broken days?

9

Fire and light
both sting.
We go to sleep when the other half
of the globe wakes up.
Night and day
crammed with dreams.

10

Your look
passes through me
like lightning.

11
The butterfly that flew by a moment ago
over the killed ones
was a soul
searching for home.

12
Our time together
has ripened, and is now
being smashed like berries.

13

Can your camera capture
fear in the eyes
of the mother sparrow, see
the broken eggs in her eyes?

14

A little air means so much for the bird.
In the air, a full world extends.
The clouds gather and then separate.
The leaves wave to each other.
For the bird, everything hangs in the air.

15
The pomegranate seeds
that scattered with our steps
were not from heaven.

16
My paper boat that drifted into the river
with the world behind it
carried a special note.
It may arrive one day,
although late,
as all truths come late.

17
Dried leaves
over there:
our first yearnings.

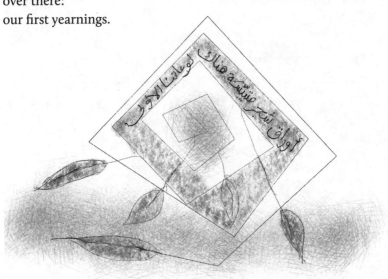

18
The shoes by the door
will not fit them when they return.

19

She counts the pebbles at her fingers.
The other pebbles underwater
become losses outside her hands.

20

Specks of sand
fell down
from the fingers:
our people.

21

The sun reveals
a hole in the boat,
a glow in the fins
of fish still breathing.

الشمس تكشف
ثقباً في سطح القارب
لمعاناً في حراشف
سمكة ما زالت تتنفّس

22

The day and the night
divide our steps on the road
as they equally
divide the world.

الليل و النهار
يقتسمان خطوّاتنا على الدرب
مثلما يقتسمان العالم
بالتساوي

23

Your hair turns gray
as you write page after page.
Trees grew
in the spaces between words
over your old steps.

24

Her shadow
is still here
feeding the birds.

Tablets III

1
Like the turtle,
I walk everywhere
with my home on my back.

2
The mirror on the wall
doesn't reflect any of the faces
that used to pass
before it.

3
The dead
act like the moon:
they leave the Earth behind
and move away.

4
Oh, little ants,
how you move forward
without looking back.
If I could only borrow your steps.

5

All of us are autumn leaves
ready to fall at any time.

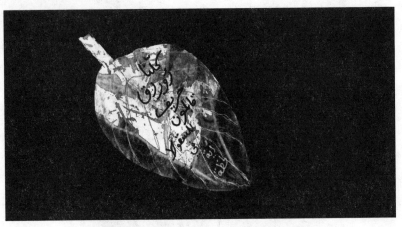

6

The spider makes a home outside itself.
It doesn't call it exile.

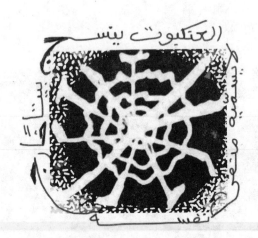

7
Forgotten
faces of the dead
as if we had only met once
through revolving doors.

8
I am not a pigeon
knowing my way home.

9
Just like that
they packed our green years
to feed hungry sheep.

10
Of course you can't see the word love.
I wrote it on water.

11

They broke your heart
and you gathered it:
an alphabet, each letter
a miniature planet
as if a light at the end of a tunnel.

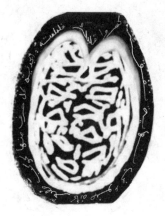

12

The grandfather left the country with one suitcase.
The father left with empty hands.
The son left with no hands.

13
No, I am not bored of you.
The moon, too, appears every day.

14
She drew her pain:
a colorful stone
settled deep inside the sea.
The fish can neither touch the stone
nor swim past it.

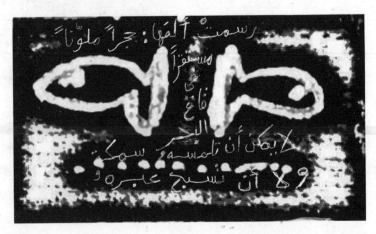

15
She was safe
inside her mother's belly.

16
The lanterns know the value of night,
and they are more patient
than the stars.
They stay until morning.

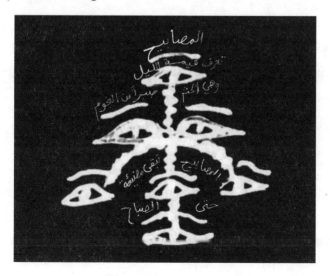

17

Those colorful flowers
over the mass graves
are the dead's last words.

18

The Earth is so simple—
you can explain it with a tear or a laugh.
The Earth is so complicated—
you need a tear or a laugh
to explain it.

19

The number you see now
will inevitably change
with the next roll of the dice.
Life won't show its faces
all at once.

20

I love you
as a singular
even though I use the plural,
both the regular and irregular plural.

21

The sweet moment is over.
I spent an hour
thinking of that moment.

22

The butterfly brings pollen
with its little feet, and flies away.
The flower can't follow it—
its leaves flutter,
and its crown grows wet
with tears.

23

Some of our tribal members
died in war, some
died regular deaths.
None of them died from joy.

24

That woman standing in the public square
is made of bronze.
She's not for sale.

Tablets IV

1

I wanted to write an epic about suffering,
but when I found a tendril
of her hair among the ruins
of her mud house,
I found my epic there.

2

I didn't sleep last night.
It was as if the night
itself hid in the morning coffee.

3

Her life is a game of snakes and ladders
sent relentlessly back to square one.
But whose life isn't like this? She takes
a breath and throws the dice again.

4

The city glitters below
the airplane window, not because
of the bones and skulls scattered
under the sun, but because of the view
through the frosted porthole.

5

She died, and time changed
for those she loved most,
but her watch kept ticking.

6

A god carried the burdens
until the weight persuaded him
to transfer them to man:
the new suffering god.

7
The map of Iraq looks like a mitten
and so does the map of Michigan—
a match I made by chance.

8
If you can't save people
at least don't hate them.

9
The first dance . . .
The first kiss . . .
The first home . . .
Words lost in translation.

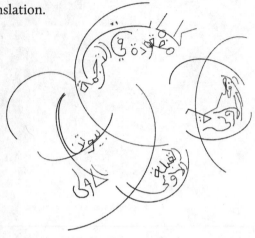

10

The city's innumerable lights
turning on and off remind us
we are born to arrive
as we are born to leave.

11

The handkerchiefs are theirs,
but the tears are ours.

12

Women running barefoot.
Behind them, stars falling from the sky.

13
So strange
that in my dream of us
you were also a dream.

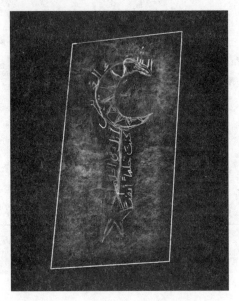

14

He said to me: You are in my eyes.
Now when he sleeps,
his eyelids cover me.

15

Gilgamesh stopped wishing
for immortality,
for only in death could he be certain
of seeing his friend Enkidu again.

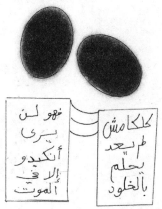

16

Some say love means
putting all your eggs
in one basket.
If they all break,
will the basket remain intact?

17

The homeless are not afraid
of missing something.
The world passes before their eyes
as clouds pass over rushing cars;
pigeons miss some of the seeds
on the road and fly away.
Yet only the homeless know
what it means to have a home
and to return to it.

18
The wind and rain
batter us
without discrimination.
We are equal
in the eyes of the storm.

19

When I was broken into fragments
you put me back together
piece by piece, like a puzzle.
I no longer fear being broken
at any moment.

20

Freezing in the mountains
without blankets or food,
and all they heard was
No news is good news.

21

Their stories didn't kill me
but I would die if I didn't
tell them to you.

22

Before killing them
they collected their personal effects.
All of their cell phones are ringing
in the box.

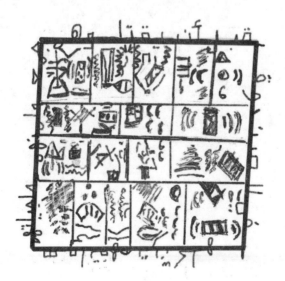

23

We are not upset when
the grass dies. We know
it will come back
in a season or two.
The dead don't come back
but they appear each season
in the greenness of the grass.

24
If yearning encircles us,
what does it mean?
That a circle has no beginning
and no end?

Tablets V

1
Light falls from her voice
and I try to catch it as the last
light of the day fades. . . .
But there is no form to touch,
no pain to trace.

2
Are dreams
taking their seats
on the night train?

3
She recites a list of wishes
to keep him from dying.

4
The truth lands like a kiss:
sometimes like a mosquito,
sometimes like a lantern.

5

Your coffee-colored skin
awakens me to the world.

6

We have only one minute
and I love you.

7
All children are poets
until they stop reaching for
butterflies that are not there.

8

The moment you thought you lost
me,
you saw me clearly
with all of my flowers,
even the dried ones.

9

If you pronounce all the letters
and vowels together at once,
you would hear each of their names
falling drop by drop
with the rain.

10

We carved
our ancestral trees into boats.
The boats sailed into harbors
that looked safe from afar.

II
Trees talk to each other
like old friends
and don't like to be interrupted.
They follow anyone who
chops one of them,
turning that person
into a lonely branch.
Is this why in Arabic
we say "cut from a tree"
when we mean
"having no one"?

والأشجار تتبادل الكلام
مثل أصدقاء قدامى
ولا تحب أن يقاطعها أحد
لذلك كل مَن يقطع شجرة
تلاحقه لعنتها فيصبح
كأنه مقطوع من شجرة

12

The way roots hide
under trees—
there are secrets,
faces, and wind
behind the colors
in Rothko's untitled canvases.

13

Will the sea forget its waves,
as the caves have forgotten us?

14
Back when there was no language
they walked until sunset
carrying red leaves
like words to remember.

قديماً عندما لم تكن هناك لغة
ساروا حتى مغيب (الشمس)
حاملين أوراق شجر
مثل كلمات عليهم تذكّرها

15
It's true that pain
is like air, available
everywhere,
but we each feel
our pain hurts the most.

صحيح أن الألم كالهواء
متوفر في كل مكان
ولكننا نظن أن ألمنا
يوجع أكثر

16

So many of them died
under stars
that don't know their names.

17

If she just survived with me.

18

A flame dims in the fireplace,
a day slips quietly away from the calendar,
and Fairuz sings, "They say love kills time
and they also say time kills love."

19

The street vendor offers tourists
necklaces with divided hearts,
shells to murmur the sea's secrets in your ear,
squishy balls to make you feel better,
and maps of homelands you fold
in your pocket as you go on your way.

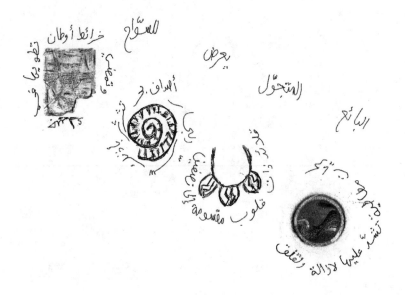

20

I am haunted by the melody
of a forgotten song
sung while two hands
tied my shoelaces into a ribbon
and waved me goodbye to school.

21

If I could photocopy
the moment we met
I would find it full
with all the days and nights

22

It won't forget the faraway child,
that city whose door stayed open
for passersby, tourists, and invaders.

23
The moon is going to the other
side of the world
to call my loved ones.

24
The seasons change
colors and you come and go.
What color is your departure?

Tablets VI

I

When the sun is absent
the flower misses her,
and when the absence grows long
the flower looks inside herself
for a different light.

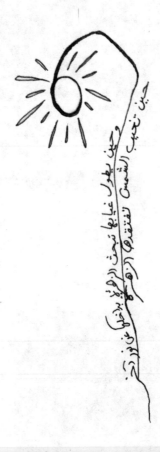

2

My flower will not wither.
It's drawn in my notebook.

3

I am the plural
who walks to you
in the singular.

4
Artificial tears
needed urgently for dry eyes.
Natural tears leaked
for centuries
into the rivers and overflowed.

5
Before you shoot someone
remember a mother's eyes
will follow you wherever you go
until she drowns you in her tears.

6
They didn't like his idea
so they shot him in the head.
Out of the bullet hole
his idea will unfurl like a climbing plant
and spread through the world.

7

Only one heart resides
in each person,
but each heart is a train
full of others who die
when that person is killed.

8

There's a sun inside each book.
Come and bring the new day
that waits for us to dawn.

9

She asked the night:
Why are you so dark?
The night answered:
So that the starlight
can reach you.

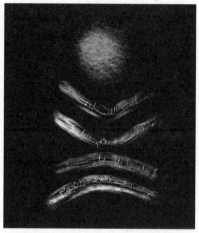

10

She asked the day:
Why don't you light up?
The day answered:
Because I've become your shadow.

11

Life is beautiful and painful
like a feather pulled
from a wing.

12

When the pistachios ripen
we break their shells
like we break open the hearts
of our lovers.

13

If thieves come to your home
let them take everything
except your dreams.
Keep those in a safe box.

14

She dreams
and her friend completes the dream.
When they separate,
the Earth rotates
more slowly
and with half the dream.

15
The trees, like us,
depend on their roots
in times of danger.

16
During the pandemic
we are a forest—trees
standing alone together

17
We watch our days—
a snowman melts away
as he should.

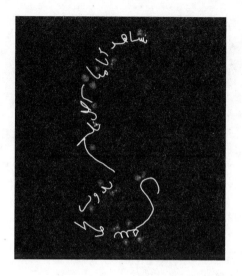

18
There are days we wait for
and they come,
and there are days that happen to us
which we cannot avoid.

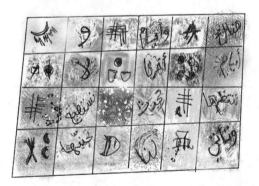

19
The bubbles in the aquarium
are the notes from the fish
about the world.

20
Like a patient teacher
the sun brightens our wrongdoings
at the same time every day.

21

When the bird
is prevented from singing,
his body turns into music
that fills the horizon.

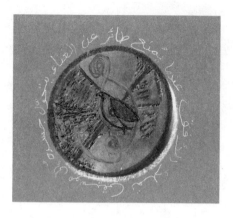

22

The birds never ask
if you are going to heaven
or hell
and they never divide the sky
into stations.

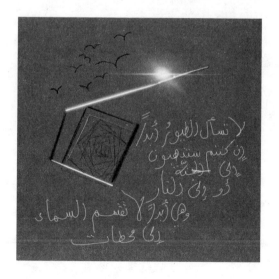

23

When the birds chirp in your head
trust their message, especially
if they say to you,
for example,
Flying is your true home.

24

What if the guns
turned into pencils
in the hands of the soldiers,
so that they can circle
all the places on the map
as sites to see before they die?

Tablets VII

1

They inscribed their lives on clay
and moved away.
Pulse after pulse I hear their echoes.

2

Some memories we chase away,
as if goats from flowers,
and yet we wake one day
to the wilted ruins.

3

Let's meet inside the word
they forgot to include in the dictionary,
and breathe its air like the smell of kleicha
my mother baked for Eid.

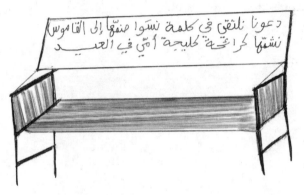

4

In my country, I was a stranger.
In exile, I am even stranger.

5
The spider built its net
in a statue's open palm.
For the spider, the palm is home
and not a metaphor for home.

6

Imprisoned in the magic lamp
for so many years, the jinni
cannot wish himself out. His freedom
is sporadic and brief, and depends
on others to wish for a bit of luck.

7

When the human cries,
the dog thinks the world is ending.
When the human smiles,
two stars from the world's end
glitter in the dog's eyes.
When the human makes war
or anything else just as ridiculous,
the dog begs to curl up together on the rug.

8

She calls aloud for the absent
in her country's air,
calling day and night
until they cling to her voice.

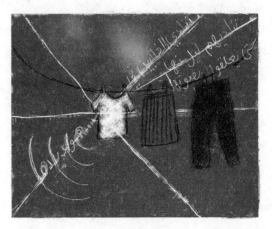

9

If you don't carry the sun
within, why does light
spill out from you?

10

In the depths of the beach,
moss grows around a rock
in a soft embrace.
When the water washes it away,
the moss trembles like the waving
gestures we make from balconies
for our loved ones during the pandemic.

11

We remember the days from the words
of the people whom we love.

12

They kept drawing circles on the ground
as if their alphabet was a feeling with no end.

13

Sometimes I scribble images
because I can't find the words.

14

I ask the moon, Which is more worthy of love,
your brightness or darkness? The moon
replies, A worthy love accepts both faces.

15

On the chess board,
a pawn crawls to the last square
to survive.

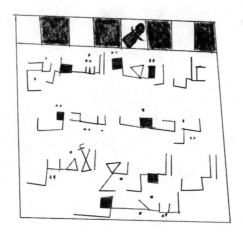

16

Earth, too, needs space.

17

I time traveled to you
for a question.

18
Through closed eyes,
she saw their stolen bodies,
their scattered feathers,
and their flutes.

19
Sad silence in every language.

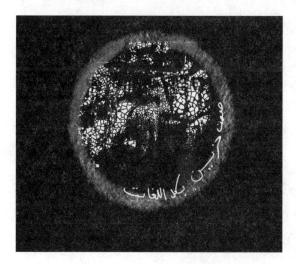

20

The first moment of war:
a fish slips out of the river.

21

The cage owner reminds the sparrow,
Life outside is an inferno.
One day the sparrow flies away
and there in the heights,
overlooking the ruins of the world,
the sparrow discovers the cage owner was right.
It sings about the ruins—
a beautiful song without walls.

22

Does the clock know
that each of its little ticks
add up to eternity?

23

With one click,
I can download your smile
and everything will be okay.

24
Let love be
the new world order.

Tablets VIII

I
Every immigrant
carries a perforated vase
that leaks nostalgia as they
very carefully walk
as if each drop
is their last breath.

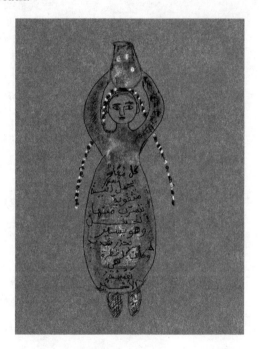

2

"The sky in my country
is more beautiful
than any other sky"—
but we fell from that sky
dream by dream
star by star.

*The quotation is a variation on Iraqi poet Badr Shakir al-Sayyab's line from his poem
"A Stranger by the Gulf" (1953): "The sun in my country is more beautiful than any other."*

3

Before we played,
I took a photograph
of my chessboard
on the table,
each wooden piece
in its designated place.
Then my father pretended I had won.
I should have let him into the picture.
When he died,
everyone was in the wrong place.

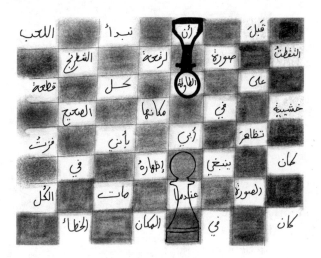

4

First one house, then another,
then a street, a temple, a village,
trees, and a creek emerge
from the holes of the flute
as she plays for the dead.

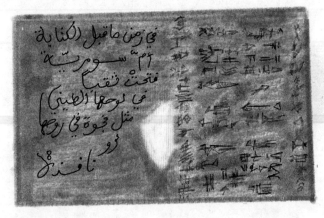

5

In the time before the invention of writing,
a Sumerian mother
opened a hole in her clay tablet
as if it were a gap in her soul,
or a window.

6

On another tablet,
she drew a vase inside a heart.
Did something fill her heart
that could not be emptied?
Is her heart a void?
Or merely a vase?

7

A clay jar on the shelf
empty and bare,
save for the traces
of the hands that formed it
then died, before eternity.

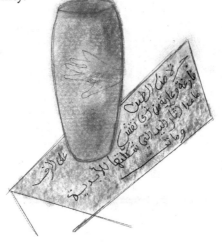

8
Each night I hear
them walking, their feet
leaving the life behind them,
shadows following shadows.
No explanation for their defeat
in this world or the underworld.

كل ليلــــة
أسمع خطواتهم
وهم يسيرون تاركين
الحياة وراءهم
ظلال خلف ظلال
لا تفسير لهزيمتهم
في هذا العالم
ولا في العالم السفلي

9

My grandfather used to say
that my grandmother was a palm date,
sweet, but with a solid pit.
Last week we found him crying
next to a dead palm tree.

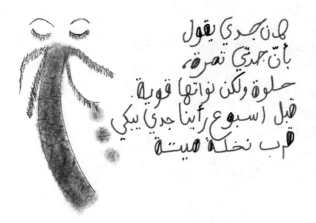

10

When I miss my friends,
I find them in tree leaves.
I see their hands waving
from swaying branches.

11

I collect flowers
to smell my life,
trying to remember
one hundred forgotten dreams.

 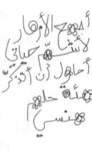

12

The most comforting maps
don't show the locations
of betrayals or regrets.

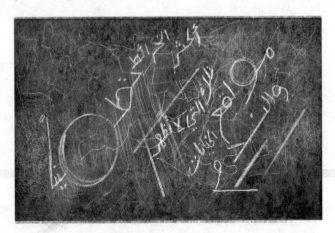

13

The endless whistling of insects
sounded like a discordant chorus
storming the field.
When I yelled at them,
they cried like babies
in a frightening world.

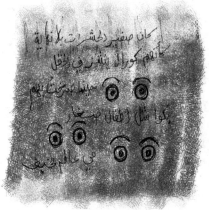

14

I don't know the name
of the dead elephant.
Her relatives surrounded her,
smelled her, examined her body
with their dexterous trunks,
and when she still didn't get up,
they lowered their heads in agony.

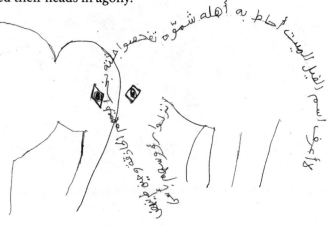

15

I play music
for the lonely flower in the vase
so she won't miss her life
in the garden.

أعزف الموسيقى
للزهرة الوحيدة في الآنية
لئلا تفتقد حياتها
في الحديقة

16

A little sparrow pecks
a single grain
and drops it.
This is how life drips
from our hourglass
grain by grain.

17
Here is a napkin
to scribble down your dreams,
and here a torch
to light the way to them.

18
You is a subject
in need of no predicate.

19

A memory of an embrace
lost in whirls of dust
spun by time, then spit out.

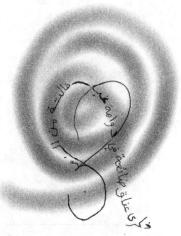

20

The smell of incense
lingers in the air
above the pile of ash
mingling with all the words
unsaid between us.

21

When you gave me a flower,
something magical happened:
Now everything I touch blooms.
The bread I eat, the car I drive,
even the broom flowers.
Now I am afraid to touch you.

22

The sun doesn't know her age.
She's older than me and you,
but every day she's born anew.
So is my love for you.

23

What did they say to each other
that couple whose glances
could move a mountain
before they became sculptures
in the park?

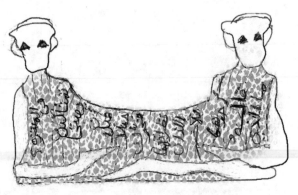

24

The way the sea believes in waves
and clouds in rain
is how the world believes in us,
and then forgets.

Tablets IX

1

I asked my dear poem
for some happy words.
She looked at me with puppy
eyes and sighed,
You decide which words are happy or sad.

2

In my old city, when someone dies,
they bring a happy word with them
to keep them company in the grave.
War after war, the happy words were used up.
I smuggled one out: imagination.

3
My Sumerian ancestors
invented the wheel,
and poetry followed—
words searching for other words
like kidnapped family.

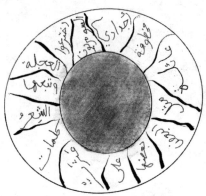

4
Poetry is love.
Prose is marriage.

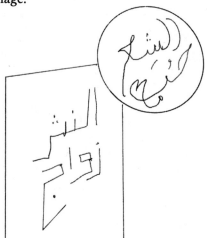

5

Prose is light.
Poetry is lightning.

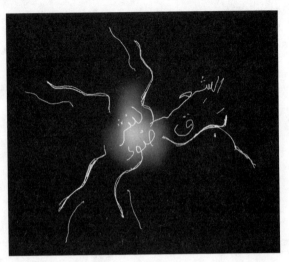

6

My poem is waiting for me
in the coffee shop, when I'm
anxious of being late, or busy
with other things. She
stares out the window,
alone and incomplete.

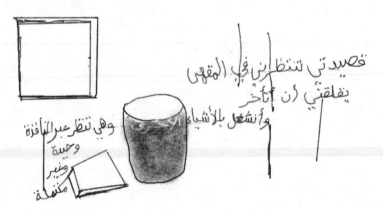

7

Unfinished poems cling to the mind
like those leaves still hanging on
after the storm.

8

I discovered poetry in a biology class—
a single amoeba cell
with an eye for witnessing
and a foot to leave tracks.

9

The form of my poem
becomes messy
when I try to describe
how I love you.

10

Nothing is better
than a good poem.
But if you read a bad poem
nothing bad happens to you.

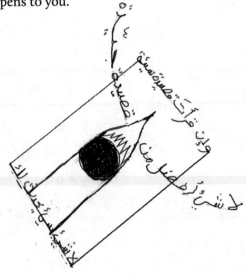

11

Poetry is how the fish discovers
the third shore of the river.

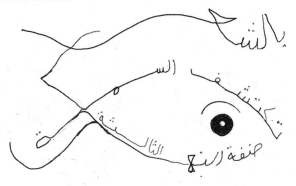

12

Some poems are complicated,
some are silly,
some are troublemakers,
but all poems have parents
who want them to do well.

13

In Italian, a stanza means "room."
In Arabic, a line of poetry, bayt, means "home."
Is this why I don't feel exiled?

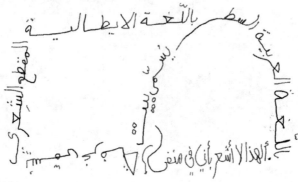

14

I picked up a pencil
to pave a poem
which became my road.

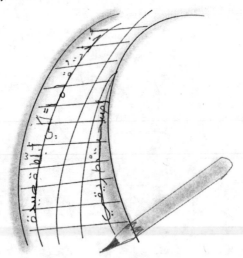

15
My dreams are usually silent
with a lot happening at once.
That's also how I wake up
from a poem.

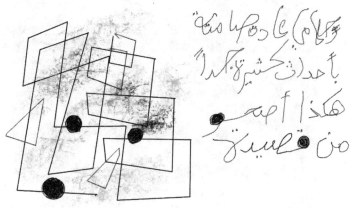

16
My poem
sometimes plays a drum
when I'm asleep.

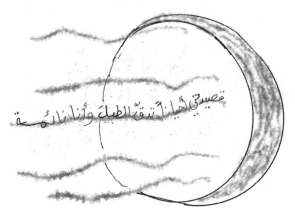

17

One hundred butterflies about to catch fire . . .
my poem startles me awake.

18

I am a citizen of poetry.
Readers migrate
to my poem
and I welcome them
as I was welcomed by others.

19
Your poem emptied into the world:
a moment touched by everyone
a bewilderment
a draft of life.

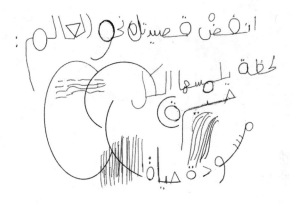

20
My poem doesn't understand
the meaning of old age.
She wants me to keep playing.

21

We ask the poem to speak
when she's still in her crib,
rocking without words.

22

Whenever I am lost,
they find me in a poem.
Poetry is my four directions.

23

Poetry isn't medicine—
it's an X-ray.

24

No finish lines
in poetry.

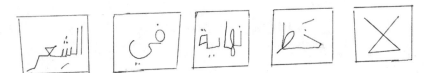

Tablets X

I
Her voice floated out
from the deepest blue
a phone could transmit:
She said: I am M . . . Remember me?
I said: I had a childhood friend named M.
She said: That's me, your childhood friend.
Where are you?
I said: Lost, and you? Where are you?
She said: Lost.
And our laughter
made the absence disappear.

جاءني صوتها دونما ساسرتني؟ أين أنت؟ قالت؟ كـ بني؟
؟ قلت: كانت لي صديقة الانخذ ... قالت؟ تلك هي ؛ صديقة طفولتك؟
أين أنت؟ قلت: ضائعة ؟ طفولة أسطورية من... صديقة
الهاتف قالت: أنا؛
وأضحكنا ضياعنا الغياب

2

We resumed our talk
that began fifty years ago
on the branches of the jujube tree
in Baghdad,
not paying attention to how the days
had spilled from our pockets.

3

The jujube tree grew old;
but we remained children,
flowering without secrets.

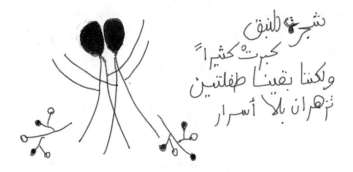

4

Once, we made a horse
out of a tree branch. We rode
the horse to faraway countries
that we had seen in picture books
so we could meet other children.
We visited their dreams
and they visited ours.
Stories grew into more stories.
Then one day we cried
because our horse branch had died.

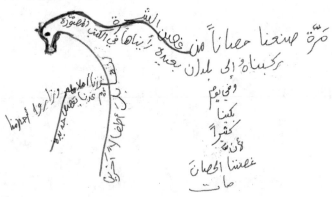

5

A wise neighbor taught us
to draw a circle around fear
to make it disappear.
My friend made two loop earrings:
one for her fear, and one for mine.

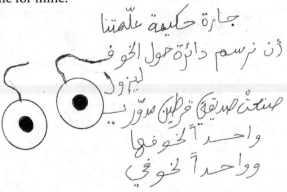

6

When the war started,
our fear grew so large
it broke our circle,
leaving us exposed
to the explosions.
We tried to encircle
its blasts with our singing.

7

When the tree heard our song,
the branches swayed in ecstasy
and chorused to us with fruit.
When the war saw us eating
the tree's music, it asked
to join in the singing.
We understood the war's hunger
and its boredom. But the war
swallowed our country whole.
We watched in shock as the war
got sicker and sicker and threw us up.

حينما سمعت الشجرة أغنيتنا
تمايلت أغصانها طربا
ومنحتنا ثمارها كورالا موسيقيا
وحين شاهدتنا الحرب
ونحن نأكل موسيقى الشجرة
طلبت أن تغني معنا
فهمنا جوعها
ومللها من الضجيج
لكنها بلعت بلدنا بأكمله
لم نصدق أعيننا
ونحن نرى الحرب تمرض أكثر
وأكثر حتى تقيأتنا

8

Away from our town,
we became the roads we had walked to school,
the always open doors,
the razqi flowers separated from their scent.

9

The emptied houses
exchanged looks
with the departed who kept
looking back.

10

We left our clothes fluttering
on the roofs of our homeland,
where our memories
must have dried by now.

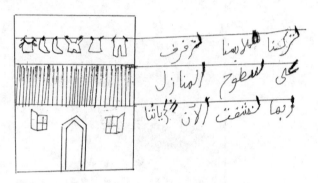

11

A bullet
then a siren
then ruins
then a bird song
telling the truth.

12

Our country is a small circle
inside a bigger circle.
Whenever we meet old friends,
the world becomes a small circle.

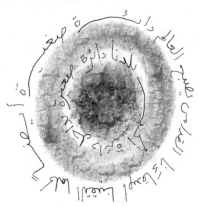

13

When we sit
at the foot of the tree
weary of searching
for home, the tree speaks:
Find your seed to reach home.

14

When my friend bowed
to let the war pass over her head,
she discovered a seed—
the globe she would roam.

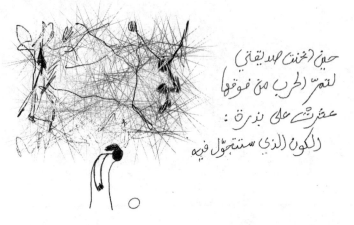

15

When I found the seed,
I discovered that my home
is not a place.

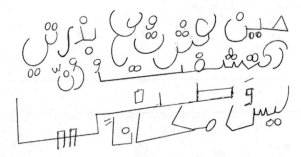

16

I need a seashell
to hear the chatter of the girls
as we walked home from school,
the clamor and claps as we jumped
on the hopscotch squares,
traces of chalks still on our hands.

17

Our footsteps follow the sun
like sunflowers, happy at sunset
for the nurturing rest of darkness,
as we bend to different stars.

18

My friend asked: When are we
meeting?
I replied: As soon as possible.
She agreed: You mean now, right?
I said: Yes!
And we laughed together.

سألتني صديقتي : متى نلتقي ؟
قلتُ : بأقرب وقت
قالت : تقصدين الآن، أليس كذلك ؟
قلتُ : نعم !
وضحكنا معاً

19

The cold day
made us silent, as we sat
on a bench overlooking the Detroit River.
Then, suddenly, a thermos
with cardamom tea and two pieces of cake
appeared from her bag,
like a rabbit from a magician's hat.

20

My friend asked: Remember
when you said you could fly,
and I believed you?
I smiled: I can still fly.

21

When I asked my friend
where we could find the stars
that we picked like jujube fruit
up on the roof those summer nights,
she pointed to the glimmer in our eyes.

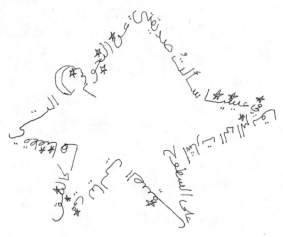

22

Where is the doll
that we picked from the toy box
as our sister, and how did we orphan her
among the ruins?

أَين تلك الدمية التي التقطناها
من صندوق الألعاب
(خِتاً لنا) ؟
كيف تركناها يتيمة
وسط الأنقاض ؟

23

I asked if every river
is the Tigris for her,
ever sadder as its waters
flow away without returning.

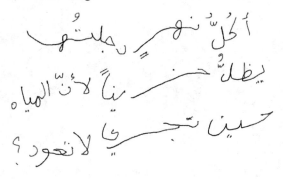

24

Every drop of water
is a different memory
of a river crossed by those
we know and don't know.
Some who have died
we hide behind our eyes.
Some who are living
we hide to keep alive.
Some who are friends
bring over the Tigris
in a cup of tea.

Dunya Mikhail is an Iraqi American poet and writer. She is the author of the poetry collections *The War Works Hard* (shortlisted for the International Griffin Poetry Prize), *Diary of a Wave Outside the Sea* (winner of the Arab American Book Award), *The Iraqi Nights* (winner of the John Frederick Nims Memorial Prize for Translation), and *In Her Feminine Sign*, which was chosen as one of the ten best poetry books of 2019 by the New York Public Library. Her nonfiction book *The Beekeeper* was a finalist for the National Book Award, and her debut novel, *The Bird Tattoo*, was shortlisted for the International Prize for Arabic Fiction. Mikhail is a laureate of the UNESCO Sharja Prize for Arab Culture and is a recipient of the UN Human Rights Award for Freedom of Writing. She currently teaches Arabic and poetry at Oakland University in Michigan.

Author photograph by B. A. Van Sise